quiet

journey

within

RHEA GUNDRATHI

i

Copyright © 2025 Rhea Gundrathi

Made with ❤ on the Notion Press Platform

www.notionpress.com

To Amma

who made this book come to reality

Dive into these pages, not just with your eyes, but with your heart—let this book take you to a place your soul has been waiting for.

<u>AUTHOR'S NOTE</u>

Dear Reader,

This book holds the beauty you crave and the pain you fear.

These poems don't just tell stories—they feel, they heal and they hurt.

This book can be your comfort or your confrontation, your truth, or your lie.

Choose wisely.

Acknowledgments

Hey Readers,

Thank you for choosing my book.
It is a piece of my soul imprinted on these dove-white pages. Holding it in your hands feels like a dream come true, and I have so many people to thank for making this possible.

To Mrs. Asfia, my inspiration and guru, who believed in me before I believed in myself.
To Tarun, whose endless enthusiasm fueled my creativity and kept me inspired.
To Suhani, who was always eager to read my drafts and cheer me on.

To my beloved parents, whose love and support have been the foundation of not just this book, but my entire life.

And, of course, to you—my incredible readers.

this is where the heart opens,

where words rise like breath on a cold morning,

fragile, fleeting, yet full of meaning.

i fight life,

i fight me,

i fight you,

and i curse myself,

when i fight back my tears

learn to swim,

because there will be a day,

when you drown,

and no one will get you back out

so, hold your breath

my parents named me rhea

a flowing river carving its path

growing deeper and deep

a ray of hope

promising that no matter how turbulent

life may get

everything will find its way

and flow far, far ahead.

sometimes be grateful

that you're not them

because once you understand

that you're not them

lot of things will start

making sense.

to be honest

i don't know how i write poems,

because at the end of the day,

the pain in my heart

is just merely being called art.

SUCCESS
STARTS
WITH
DISCIPLINE

breaking is just a chapter of life

even the greatest ships have sunk

yet they now rest in museums-

their stories etched in the hearts of those who

remember

in short.

three boys. father. killer beast.

dad sent the first son to defeat the dragon,

the first son failed, hence died.

second son, also dead

third son, the youngest and the wisest,

dead.

now you tell me,

who killed all the sons,

the father or the beast?

the difference between me and you

is not

looks

speech

speed

followers

it is the way we think.

the more you face the truth
the more they'll tear through you
they'll burn, they'll scar, they'll break you

face it anyway.

sometimes,

just sometimes

i wish i was someone else's poem,

not the poet.

together
FOREVER

it is you i would die for,

so, can i be the one you live for?

if you ever loved someone as much as

the sun loves the day,

and they shattered your heart

i hope life serves them

the pain so deep

they never forget the sound

of your breaking.

i crave to be someone's priority

but the voices in me

know that's too much to expect

from anyone but myself.

it hurts me to know that you will never care about me

the way i care about you.

kindness can be a person

but it's tragic

how that person has never been you

my words are like hopeless thorns

they tear you before they bloom

leaving scars

and dripping blood

and i forget to pause,

to breathe.

is it really that hard

for people to understand that

i am not them,

if you want the rest of us

to be the same

why bother having

eight billion people?

my house maybe a

a village

a hut

a flat

or a building

but my home belongs in just one place,

it's where you are.

it's sad how everything beautiful

will always be less beautiful than you.

Rhea Gundrathi

not every shooting star is meant to grant your wish

i had told you how much

they all made me overthink

and you left me feeling the same way.

life may not be treating you

easy right now

but there are enough poems in this

book to make sure that

you will be okay.

isn't it amazingly

astonishingly

unbelievingly

surprising how those little sounds from your throat

in this carbon filled world,

those little marks on the dove white sheet

can carry the weight of silence,
speak louder than actions,
leave echoes that linger in the mind

can both heal and harm,
build bridges or walls?

word are weapons,

for they carve through the soul.

we are writers

we do not speak what we think

we pour

onto these very pages

the same pages you flip through

not realizing that they hold

the weight of everything

we never say aloud.

when someone asks me

what i fear the most,

it's not the things that have never happened

it's the things that i fear will

happen again...

the show is over,

why are you still acting?

my laugh, my smile-

just a beautiful lie,

a mask i wear

as i slowly die inside.

who am i

when i'm alone?

embrace the unknown

let fear dissolve

for in this moment

we are reborn

she buried the little girl

she once was

deep inside the mud

and cried hysterically next to her grave

wait,

why is there mud on my hands?

the painting I display of myself

may convince you

that you know me well.

but keep in mind

i am the artist behind it.

the monster in my head

won't let me flee

monster, monster so you see

this is what you have done to me

i hear your voice with every breathe

a quite promise of regret and death

no matter how much I try to run

you remind me

that we are one.

to prosper i will need these for now;

a pen and a page.

sometimes the last thing

you need is

people

Just sometimes.

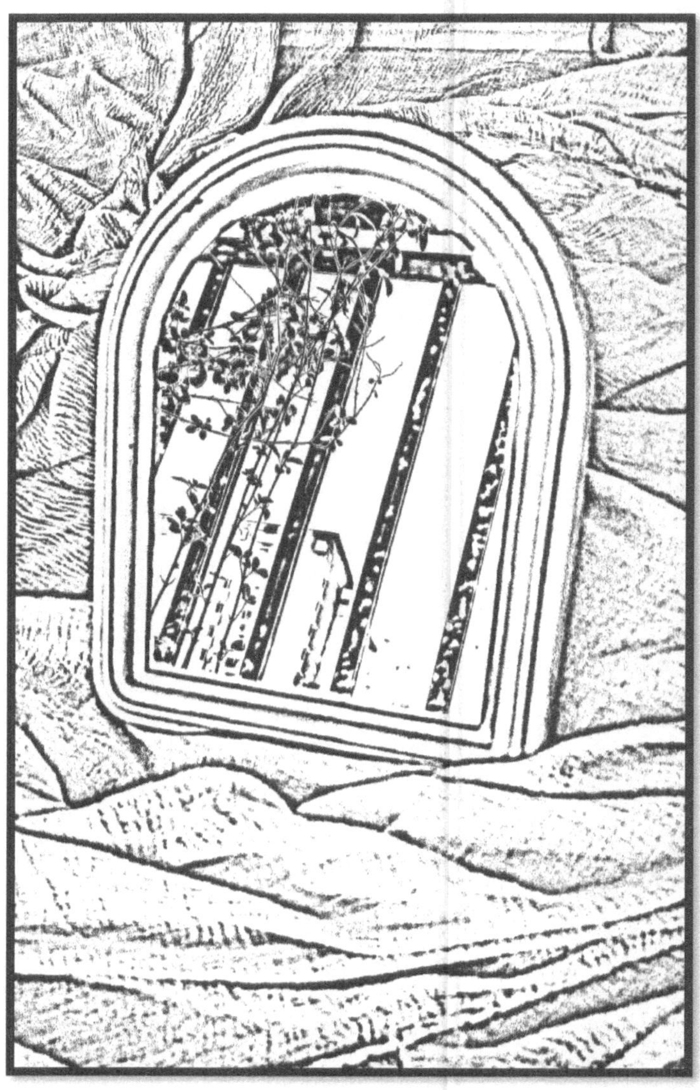

i looked at my tear-stained

face glance back at me from the mirror

the mirror was shattered

or maybe it was just me.

do not say I deserve better

instead

be that 'better'

someone who overthinks

is someone who

over loves

over cares

and overall is superior feelings-wise.

most people hate their anger

but i love mine

and it loves me back enough

to let me know my self-worth

Rhea Gundrathi

once in a while

i choose devils

over angels

do not expect a lot

from anyone

just because you would

do that for them

it's still open

torn at the edges

a place where the hurt sinks in

again

and again

and again.

will you please just let the wound heal?

NEVER
NEVER
NEVER
GiVE UP

you spent years building that character—

maybe 15,

maybe more.

don't let anyone destroy it in 15 seconds.

i am so desperate

to feel the same childishness

and joy i once left

to the point where i make things up

in my head

so maybe

i made us up.

scars don't define,

they only show

how far you have come

and how much you will grow.

it lives in my heart

strangled tight around my lungs

making each breath a struggle

a weight I cannot let go

the silence pulls me deeper and i wonder

if this wound were destined to stay exposed

and i was made to bleed endlessly

i can't breathe

or maybe I was never meant to.

i hope all the tears

of the silent voices out there

are evaporated into clouds

and rain to form flowers

that bloom into our hearts.

12
11
1
10
2
9
3
8
QUARTZ
4
7
5
6

give it time

the thoughts will pour out

and so will the pain

i don't get how

people who hurt others deeply

do not regret it

does it not keep knocking you in the head

and tingling through your veins,

that feeling of guilt?

knowing that someone isn't okay because of you

and can't sleep at night without shedding

tears that flow like rivers?

how do you hurt something that

pumps blood,

pumps life into us

so easily?

i am like the sky

vast and free

yet i'm cornered by the horizons that i can't see

i stand tall

but they stand taller

i am pretty

but they are gorgeous

i am happy

but they are joyful

if i keep comparing myself to you

tell me,

would I even remember what it feels like to stand tall,
to feel beautiful,
to hold onto happiness that's mine?

Rhea Gundrathi

the words i am

unable to speak

strangle me tight from the inside

why can't i say them?

and then i do.

but i must be doing

something wrong

for they always escape from my eyes,

never the mouth.

may you find happiness

while the sunshine nourishes your soul.

i like it,

when the sky wears the colour

of my thoughts

it's comforting to know

that something so vast

so infinite

understands me

in a world where

a few billion people couldn't.

i must be real fun to hurt

because every time

i dodge a bullet

i get stabbed in the back.

when you look at someone

and feel that burn in your chest

remember,

even the sun and moon

have their own time to shine

my cheekbones sit high

and my hair as wavy

as the chaos in my thoughts

the chocolate hue in my eyes

and my lightly pigmented lips

all so common, so very.

my appearance isn't special

but i don't mind

because what truly sets me apart

is my thoughts, words and actions

Be
Happy

things are going to be okay

and if they aren't

you haven't waited long enough

i now despise the word 'sorry'

for it is now just a word

that has no meaning

Rhea Gundrathi

it hurts

when you are falling apart

and they spit words

like shards of glass slowly

tearing through your skin

leaving wounds so deep

you can never forget them

no remedy can heal them

no cure can take away the pain

the blood i lost won't come back

sometimes i wish

someone held my hand

and told me that

everything will be okay.

how can the beginning start

when you already believe it is the end?

her every moment, beautiful.

as if she planned out her every smile

every twitch

every shiver

makes me want to melt

the way she moves her hair from her face

and gently tucks it behind her ear makes

me breathless

every hand gesture possesses a story with

an elegance of its own

{a woman}

don't you just love those days?

when the sun tells you

that everything will be okay

when the wind runs through your hair

whispering that your worries

will go away in a breeze

when the aroma of the rain's essence

on the soil holds you close

and comforts you?

when nature holds your hand tight when

none of them could?

Rhea Gundrathi

i am often called a tomboy

a girl who's like a boy

but i don't see it

the difference between

a girl and a tomboy isn't

in looks, actions,

dressing, thoughts

or an interest in cars

it shifts based on how society choses to judge.

the phrase that is

frequently

factually

completely

incorrect is 'yes, i'm okay'

hold on,

laugh, live and love

the order will change

so just

hold on

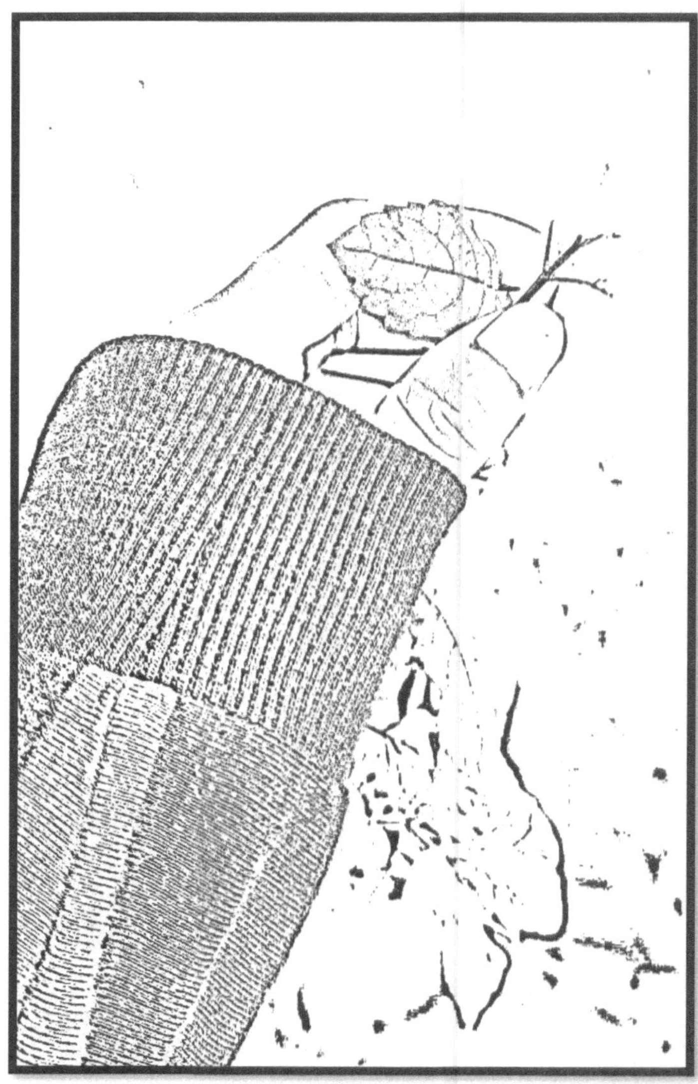

healing takes time

flowers don't bloom overnight

no one is a waste of time

take the chance to learn

how to be

and to not be

this is the youngest

you will ever be

and as you read every word

in this poem

you are ageing,

but at the same time

learning and realizing

something new

i hate the locket you gave me

so i threw it away in the trash

and now it comfortably sits in my closet

with the other pieces

of scrap you gave me

thunder may not strike twice

but you can

in a world full of

instagram, snapchat, youtube

and other social distractions

it's good to know

that people like you and me

still remember the fragrance

of books

butterflies are such heartwarming creatures

small and pretty

pigmented with colours of grace,

warmth and elegance

but not everyone favours them

some even despise them enough to hurt them

this is not about butterflies

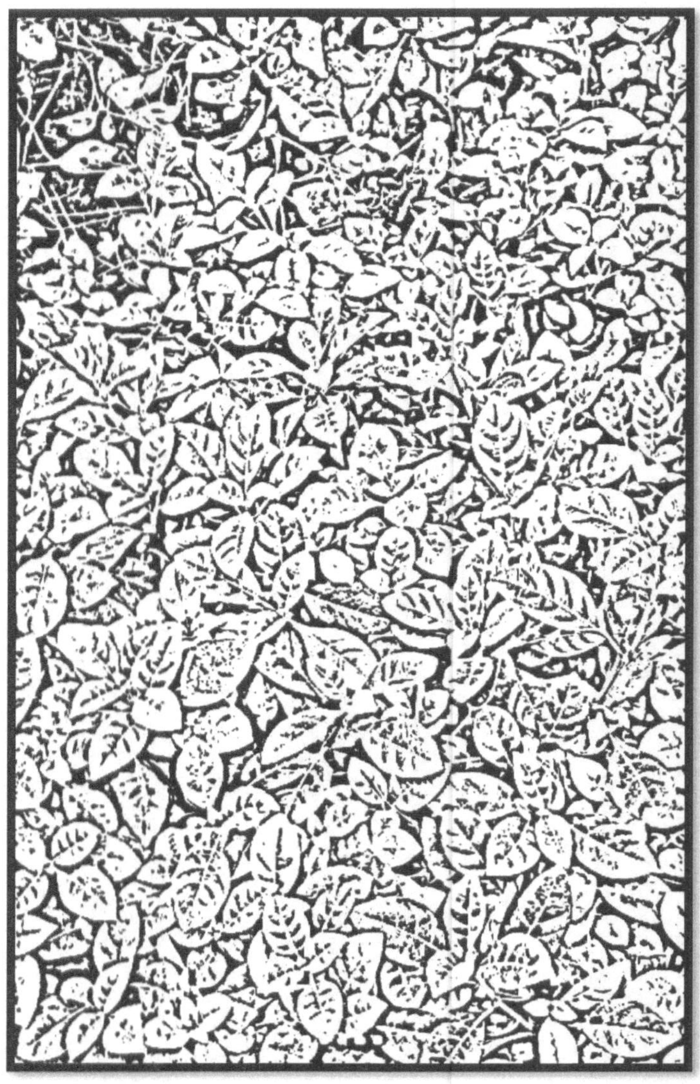

nature can be cruel sometimes

it transfers the dewdrops into our eyes

and the fog into our thoughts

but somehow

the thunders into their voice

in this world full

of petals

i wish to be a *bouquet*

where should I go?

to the right where nothing seems right,

or to the left where nothing is left?

where would you go?

left, or right?

people write when there's no one there to listen.

i want to feel as loved

as much as the stars do to the sky

when i'm not here

i don't want people to gather around

my grave for formality

come because you love me

don't put flowers that will wither away

bring the moments we shared instead

i am there

not under the stone

but in spaces of your heart.

i no longer have

butterflies in my stomach

all of them are dead.

loneliness is like fire

which I hold close to my heart

to see how much pain

i can stand

before I get burnt and run away.

the most frequently used lie

that i say is that i'm okay

no i'm not, can you not see

the regret in my eyes?

the grip in my fists

that are eagerly waiting to feel you

on their knuckles?

i often comfort others with the words

i long to hear

on some days

i lay in bed

hoping that i fall alseep

and not fall apart

sometimes i wonder

not about memes or insta

or tiktok

but about life

about reality

so question it

question reality.

you cannot

hurt someone

who is numb to the pain

as they can no longer feel it

because they've felt it too much

and too deeply

i'm sick of

all my friendships being lessons

i just wanted a companion

is that too much to ask for?

why do you have no compassion?

do i really deserve this aggression?

there was no feeling of loneliness

till there was you

my thoughts scatter

horrifyingly

when i need them

the most

Hope these words ran through your veins and stayed
with you,

thank you for being a part of my journey.

About the Author

Rhea Gundrathi is a teenage writer with a talent for weaving emotions into words.

You can connect with her on Instagram at @_rhea.poetry_